Revealing Who You Are

7 Chapters of Complete Happiness

Happy Reading

Kwesha D. Neal

Kwesha D. Neal

Revealing Who You Are
www.Revealwhoyouare.com

ISBN-13: 978-1974507276

Limits of Liability and Disclaimer of Warranty
The author and publisher shall not be liable for your misuse of the enclosed material. This book is strictly for informational and educational purposes only.

Warning – Disclaimer
The purpose of this book is to educate and entertain. The author and/or publisher do not guarantee that anyone following these techniques, suggestions, tips, ideas, or strategies will become successful. The author and/or publisher shall have neither liability nor responsibility to anyone with respect to any loss or damage caused, or alleged to be caused, directly or indirectly by the information contained in this book.

Medical Disclaimer
The medical or health information in this book is provided as an information resource only, and is not to be used or relied on for any diagnostic or treatment purposes. This information is not intended to be patient education, does not create any patient-physician relationship, and should not be used as a substitute for professional diagnosis and treatment.

Publisher
10-10-10 Publishing
Markham, ON
Canada

Printed in Canada and the United States of America

Table of Contents

DEDICATION

This book is dedicated to the loving memory of Brook Neal, my father, who instilled in his children that a quitter never wins, and to Louise Neal my mother — thanks for being great parents.

FOREWORD

Revealing Who You Are is an eye-opener, which allows you to see the importance of looking into yourself, to find the real you. It will help you define yourself, and your purpose in life.

Author Kwesha Neal shows you how to tap in to your own glory, pulling back toxic layers of low self-esteem and regret. It gives you a reason to move forward.

Reading this book will give you courage, and you will come to understand why you are so unique. It will give you clarity about why things happen the way they do, and provide you with the tools for coping, no matter what the circumstance.

You will discover why it is important to be your own best friend, and put yourself first. Read this book, and learn how to WOW yourself to happiness.

Raymond Aaron
New York Times Bestselling Author

ACKNOWLEDGEMENTS

Thank you, Milton Neal, my brother; because of you, I have life. You saved me from a devastating fire that almost led me to my death. You were at the right place at the right time. This why my life is possible. With deep love, and thanks to you, I'm able to share my story to the world.

To my sister, Loretta Nunoo: thank you for taking care of me and Mark when mom was sick in the hospital for months. I was only 3 years old, and Mark was 1. You sacrificed at an early age so that we could keep the family balanced, and you still completed your high school education on time. Dad could work and provide for the family—thanks for being my sister/mother at the time of need.

Mildred Chin-quee (Cookie): thank you, my sister. You are always willing to help a person in need. You are the first to volunteer your services to help others.

Mark Anthony Neal: my brother who always gives me encouraging words to step out on faith to be your own boss.

Harold Obie Jr., my uncle and the matriarch of the family, who strengthens the family bond and who has the listening ear and strong values—you upheld the family legacy from generation to generation.

Douglas Martin Jr., a special friend who encouraged me to continue this book—I will value your friendship forever. Thank you.

Leroy Curtis, a lifetime friend, thanks for being my mentor.

To my family and friends: thanks for all your support and for cheering me on to complete my first book. Thank you; I love you all.

Cara Witvoet, my personal book architect, thank you for your support, for being there for me, and answering my questions throughout this process.

Raymond Aaron, it has been a pleasure working with you on my book. Without you, this book would not have come to fruition. Thank you for your skill and for coaching me; you are truly the REAL Raymond.

Chapter 1

It's All About You

THE PERFECT DNA

I am in awe of the beauty when thinking about our creation of life, from a tiny sperm to an embryo. This is our first journey in life, and it is just amazing how those little cells revolved into who you are today. Our body was created with everything we need for a lifetime.

The entire earth was waiting for you on your day. It was your day to arrive to see your identity and, on that day, you were welcomed by your mother, father, grandparents, aunts, uncles, cousin, and friends—a celebration for a new beginning of life and love.

As a human, you have five senses: sight, hearing, taste, smell, and touch. They will be noticed and used from the first day of life.

These are great gifts that we have received from God, which will enhance your life. Let's discuss the five senses, one by one, to appreciate ourselves in more detail.

The human eye helps provide three dimensional moving images and normal colours in daylight. Rod and cone cells in the retina allow conscious light perception.

The human eye can see as far 2 miles, or more than 2 million light years. By the time we reach 80 years of age, we will have blinked our eyes 448,512,000 times.

With those beautiful eyes, you are able to see mountains, valleys, birds, and all the beauty of this earth.

The frequency range for hearing of a young person is about 20 to 20,000 hertz; as you get older, the highest frequency is 12 to 14 kilo hertz. Your ears never stop hearing, even when you are asleep. Your brain just ignores incoming sound—hearing the birds sing to you on a beautiful, sunny morning or hearing some loud thunder claps, miles away.

Our taste buds are housed on papillae of the tongue, where taste receptors are able to detect different chemicals. The human tongue has 3,000 to 10,000 taste buds. Each taste bud is about 0.03 millimeter in diameter and about 0.06 millimeter long. With your taste, you are able to indulge in the many different fruits and vegetables, and the tastes of different foods, e.g., American, Italian, Indian, etc.

Many people think smelling begins in the front of the nose, but that is not true. It begins in the back of the nose where millions of sensory neurons lie in a strip of tissue called the olfactory epithelium, which is about 9cm² (3 centimeters by 3centimeters) and lies on the roof of the nasal cavity, about 7cm above and behind the nostrils. The sense of smell allows you to enjoy the aroma of hot apple pie and the smell of fresh air.

The human skin is the outer covering of the body. In humans, it is the largest organ of the integumentary system. The skin has up seven layers of ectodermal tissues that guard the underlying muscles, bones, ligaments, and internal organs.

Our skin is very soft and, as we age, it may wrinkle.

Before we go any farther, let us thank our parents for the creation of life.

You can see human life start off beautifully with no flaws or errors. As you get older, you become the producer, director, and writer of your life—many uncertainties happen.

WHO YOU ARE NOT

You Are Not How You Feel

When you are upset or are having an unhappy day when everything goes wrong and you are not balanced, these are not your true emotions; it is just your emotions with those current situations. Emotions may come or go, like the day of the week or like the weather. You are much greater than your emotions.

What About Your Thinking?

Our thinking plays a major part in our thought process. We are not our thoughts. Our thoughts are more than what we really think of ourselves.

What About Things You Put Off Until Tomorrow?

I am not that person who procrastinates and puts off what I can do today until tomorrow. I create a detailed timeline with a specific deadline.

LAYERS OF YOU

1. Who are you?

What is your strength? Knowing your abilities and positive traits will boost your confidence. For example, everyone has various gifts; some are good at playing a musical instrument, or cooking, or working with their hands.

2. What are your weaknesses?

Just as the chain is only as strong as its weakest link, don't get discouraged about whatever weakness you may have. You keep practicing until you eventually get to where you are satisfied. Don't be hard on yourself because nobody is perfect on this earth and never will be.

3. What are your goals?

Why must you have a goal in your life? By doing so, you have direction, structure, and purpose. If you have a goal, you are more likely to stay on your path in life, and achieve some form accomplishment in life. Start writing some of your goals that you would like to achieve.

4. What is your strength within?

You are a child of God. He gave you the ability to live with resilience, integrity, and wisdom on this journey of life, to accept all your setbacks with a comeback, and to love yourself unconditionally.

WHAT IS YOUR PURPOSE?

The word *purpose* means the reason for which you were created or why something exists. Reread it: THE WORD *PURPOSE* MEANS THE REASON FOR WHICH YOU WERE CREATED OR WHY SOMETHING EXISTS. This meaning is personal for you and me, and is something for you to meditate and reflect on with your inner self: Where am I going? Where do I see myself? Is this current life for me? Am I disconnected from the universe and the meaning of life? But the most important question is: What is my *purpose* in life? There will never be another one of you.

If you don't have a purpose in life, you are just hanging around the earth, twiddling your thumbs, with no sense of fulfillment of life. Life purpose is a deep and personal aspect of one's meaning of life. Most people fill their lives with dissatisfaction with themselves or worrying about what happened 5 or 10 years ago, as well as worrying about other people, whose lives are none of your concern. Life purpose is not a job. It is estimated that 80% of people go to a job they don't like. They get up with the alarm clock because they are not excited about going. They can wait to leave and can't wait for the weekend. They are just making themselves sick, physically and mentally; it plays a big part in your health, e.g., high blood pressure, diabetes, etc.

Your environment also plays a big part in your health.

It was not in your DNA to feel pain, be sick, or be unhappy betraying oneself. Many people live this type of life, and the saddest part of it is that they retired with 80,000 work hours or more on a job that didn't bring them complete happiness—because they didn't find their purpose.

Ask yourself: is this me? If so, what can I do to change it?

A NEW MINDSET

Once you let go of these distractions, you can start being a *new you.* And once you establish a set of new attitudes held by you, and clean your soul of other people's waste, then your mind, body, and soul will feel clear—the clarity and translucency of *ah!* This was in your DNA the whole time. You and I were born with it.

Then, you begin to find your purpose; you have time to meditate, to research yourself, and expose all of your unknowns of you. God is giving you this gift of opportunity.

Once you master your purpose, it will become a natural ability. Your requirement becomes effortless; it doesn't require you to hesitate, stutter, or feel embarrassed.

You have found your purpose—inside your body— rejoice with new-found happiness and confidence. It is light to the heart, which makes it happy. By working with a purpose, you see progress in abundance. It is not a job; it is your purpose. When you find your purpose, you begin to live a life of good health and spiritual wealth.

Go find your purpose; we all live with one. Say it with me: MY PURPOSE, MY PURPOSE, MY PURPOSE.

For more information, go to
www.Revealingwhoyouare.com

"Everyone has a purpose in life and a unique talent to give to others. And when we blend this unique talent with service to others, we experience the ecstasy and exultation of our own spirit, which is the ultimate goal."

– Kallam Anji Reddy

Close your eyes and think of what your purpose is; dig to the pit of your stomach. You may have to come back to this page several times. Please complete this exercise because this is key to opening up your new identity.

WHAT IS YOUR PASSION?

Throughout our lives, we were told to follow our passion, or we were asked what our passion was. We heard this from great leaders of the world, or at church, graduation, or during an interview. But is that a theory or fact?

UNDERSTANDING WHAT PASSION IS

People fail to realize that passion is an emotion or feeling. Every day of our lives, our feelings about our job, hobbies, and relationships with people, change. We even feel different about the foods we buy (organic/non-organic). We also care if we purchase energy efficiency or non-energy efficiency items. Your passion can change; passion is a full forecast of energy at a current time.

The answer to the previous question: passion is a theory.

We have all heard of that old saying: just because you're passionate about something doesn't mean you are good at it.

KEEP THE DOOR OPEN

If you are always looking for passion, you may miss many opportunities. Each day, people see something in you that you don't see in yourself. For example, what if you were speaking to a producer and, while you were talking to him/her, they were watching your body movements and features. You were asked whether you had ever worked as an actress before; you said, "NO." The producer gave you his/her business card and told you they were looking for someone of your character to act in a major Broadway play in New York. How would you feel once you left that person? You would feel good about yourself and couldn't wait to tell someone.

Never follow your passion; just bring it with you, it is good company with a purpose.

For more information, go to
www.Revealingwhoyouare.com

"My mission in life is not merely to survive, but to thrive; and to do so with some passion, some compassion, some humor, and some style."

– Maya Angelou

LACK OF SELF CONFIDENCE

A secret that people keep inside, and fail to use, is confidence within themselves.

They are shy, or feel unworthy to join in conversation or to use authority.

It takes time to overcome a lack of self-confidence, but it can be done. There are many nerves in the body; you have to build them up. You must say to yourself, and believe, that if someone else can do it, you can too. It is a gradual process, but have it in your heart that you would like to do this or that.   And don't worry about anyone saying that you have some nerve; just say, "YES, I DO." And just ask for whatever you want. The bible says to ask and it shall be given. It may not work the first time, but do it again and again. Repetition and practice makes perfect. Now that you know how to build your self-confidence, go for it.

Thomas Edison had a dream to become an inventor. By the time he died on October 18, 1931, Thomas Edison had amassed a record 1093 patents: 389 for electric light and power; 195 for the phonograph; 150 for the telegraph; 141 for storage batteries; and 34 for the telephone. Thomas Edison didn't let his lack of education let his self-confidence deter him.

> *"I have not failed. I've just found*
> *10,000 ways that won't work."*
> – Thomas A. Edison

> *"One important key to success is self-confidence. An important key to self-confidence is preparation."*
> – Arthur Ashe

A LOW SELF ESTEEM

A global problem around the world is low self-esteem from the growing number of social media popping up, such as Facebook, Snapchat, Twitter. Why is self-esteem at the lowest ever? It starts early in life; are you surprised? The three words, *YOU ARE BAD,* are told to some babies early in life, and many kids hear this until adulthood. Some people with low self-esteem have been scarred for life. It is estimated that 85% of people in the world suffer from low self-esteem. This is when an individual, for some reason or other, doesn't find the love and happiness they truly are worthy of. They like certain pictures on social media, and then their friends call them haters or disconnect their friendship with them. We all want to be liked and loved, and be able to share our opinion with our friends and family.

A NEW SELF ESTEEM

Once you acknowledge that this low self-esteem just doesn't work for you, give it to God; ask him to unveil your new identity. This can be done through prayer and by talking to him just as if he were a friend you were talking on the phone with. He hears you cry and sees your wounds. God told us to ask and he will give to his kids. If nobody cares, we know that God cares about you. He will guide all in the right direction. Remember: at the end of every rainbow, there is a pot of gold. This new self-esteem will grant the fulfillment of love, safety, and the security of living in peace with yourself.

"When I loved myself enough, I began leaving whatever wasn't healthy. This meant people, jobs, my own beliefs and habits—anything that kept me small. My judgement called it disloyal. Now I see it as self-loving."
– Kim McMillen

On this paper, list some things you need to work on for your self-esteem.

NOTES

NOTES

NOTES

NOTES

Chapter 2

Happiness Within You

IS HAPPINESS MATERIAL THINGS?

Happiness—everybody wants it. They look for happiness through career, entertainment, cars, or people. But all these things are just temporary fixes. For example, what if you get your dream job and, after you have been employed there for over 5 years, the company informs you that they are outsourcing your position. Would this bring you happiness? No, it would not.

What if you received two NFL football tickets? Your favorite team is playing and you are sitting in the front row at the 50 yard line, which gives you a spectacular view of your team. Your team loses the game—that's not happiness either.

What if you purchased a Lamborghini? This was your dream car, but the transmission starts to slip after

50,000 miles. Would this bring you happiness, or would you be pissed off?

What about our friends? Some are friends for certain reasons—when you really need them, they are not there for you, and this makes you feel disappointed.

The truth of the matter is, things don't bring you happiness; material things get old, rusted, or obsolete.

Unhappiness is a big disease that human beings have. Unhappy people are not successful, and no amount of money and achievement will change the equation.

HOW TO FIND TRUE HAPPINESS

Happiness—where do you start? It starts with *you*. To be truly happy and content, I stress to my clients that they must reflect on what is making them unhappy. This is the first step.

Once you reflect on what is making you unhappy, work on it; this is the second step. In time, you will see a change in your life. Your happiness is all that matters. Understanding what makes you happy is your personal decision, and it fits you alone.

The bottom line, once you reveal your happiness, is that you never get tired of being happy. Every day, happiness gives you a life of satisfaction, leaving you hungering for more. Once you begin a journey of happiness, life's everyday problems will be an easier challenge. You will be able to say, "I can handle it."

Here are some requirements required for happiness, which I advise to my clients:

- Peace within yourself.
- Loving family and friends.
- Good health.
- Purpose in life.
- See yourself with a better future.

For more information, go to
Revealingwhoyouare.com

*"Ever more people today have the means to live,
but no meaning to live for."*
– Viktor E. Frankl

Here are some new words to master in your life, which will come with your emotions of happiness:

- agreeable
- accepting
- adore
- bliss
- cheer
- contented
- delectation
- delight
- elation
- enchantment
- enjoyment
- enthusiastic
- gaiety
- geniality
- gladness
- glee
- good cheer
- hilarity
- joviality
- joy
- laughter
- optimism
- peace of mind
- pleasure
- rejoicing
- sanctity
- well-being

LOVE YOURSELF

To my students in my workshop and lectures, I stress the point of loving yourself first as being a priority— loving yourself is a miracle cure; loving yourself works miracles in our lives. Who else is going to love you first? The 1st step in loving yourself is to examine everything about yourself, and be absolutely satisfied with *you*. Accept all your flaws and your past mistakes, and whether you are fat, skinny, have brown skin or white, are a single parent or not—just accept yourself.

The 2nd step is to look in the mirror at yourself; tell yourself that you love yourself, and see the beauty of this wonderful person that the mirror is reflecting. As you stare into the mirror, tell yourself you are the only person on the earth that you truly know for sure.

Love yourself in a way that fills your heart with overflowing, like the river; tell yourself why you love yourself.

- The joy of being alive.
- The beauty I see.
- Your smile.
- Our bodies and the wonders of how it works.

The bible says the greatest gift is love. Tell yourself we are stuck together, and we are going to have fun sharing this experience of love. People are going to see the love on the outside, and I am going to feel the love on the inside. People are going to be attracted to you because of your love and the energy you show. Loving yourself is kind; loving yourself is compassion.

"First of all, you need to love yourself because that's the only way you're going to get by and be OK as an individual. But it's also important to make other people feel loved because you never know what they're going through."
 – Sofia Richie

Take a few minutes and list all the things you love about yourself.

YOUR GIFT

We are going to talk about something more important than money. In fact, you cannot even buy it with money; this is more precious than diamonds, gold, silver, or copper. Are you puzzled? You may ask if this thing is love. Love is good; we treasure the love of our family and friends. You cannot imagine living without love. We all need love, but people fall in love and out of love.

It is values that are more important than money and love. Values are something more important than your feelings because they are something you hold deep within yourself.

What do you believe in? What is important to you? All things that you hope for, believe and care about, and are stored within yourself, are your personal values.

Always incorporate your values in all the decisions you make. Living and standing by your values helps you gain success.

Core values include peace, good health, respect, honesty, security, comfort, and loyalty. What do you value most in your life?

EXAMINING YOUR VALUES

1. Create a list of value words that speak to you.

2. Write down 4 to 9 words from your previous list that speak to you.

3. Rank them in order that is most important to you.

4. Take the 4 most important words that speak to you and put your value into practice.

NOTES

NOTES

NOTES

NOTES

NOTES

Chapter 3

Fear Not

FEAR NOT

Let me introduce you to one of your worst friends that live with you: Fear. It's like the Grinch that spoils and puts a damper on Christmas; it robs you of your joy, your mood, and your real self. It makes you upset and disappointed, yet you still fear. Is this real, true happiness, or is this nothing but anxiety or apprehension? How many times do we look at ourselves and know we can a do better, or you have said, "I am going to do better. I am going to be the little bird to tell you that you have to feel the fear. The more you achieve in life by feeling fear, the more you will fear. For one thing, you are going have to fight the fear; you have to rip off some of your layers of fear that are toxic and contaminated, so that you can breathe and smell the crisp freshness of the air. There is a time when you have to say, "I can handle the fear." We will be taking fear with us to board meetings and worship, and we will be having fun with our fear, so buckle up; I am bringing a special guest—fear. So let's define fear with a new acronym: Fire, Eager, Anticipate, Results.

Fear of moving ahead

With the economic changes in life and the computer industry moving at the speed of light, we have people that are scared to expose themselves in order to move ahead. What is keeping you in the *sea of sameness*? "I refuse to come out of my comfort zone, even though I hate certain things in my life," or "if it's not broke, don't fix it." A lot of the time, people are walking around with a broken heart, wanting to expose their true potential but not knowing what people will say. Or the outcome is not a success. In life, every human is affected by life's situations and the unpleasant emotions from different causes of pain. We were put on this earth to multiply, and subdue the earth. Our lives have real meaning; you are not just some object. Let me give you an example: earth was made eons ago. Who would ever have thought that man would walk on the moon? Or that you can skype and see people in another country. You have great potential—unleash it.

Expose your hiding potential

To live a life full of potential, your life is counting on you to find a way of doing it. This is your own personal viewpoint of yourself and nobody knows it yet. By living life with potential, there are no boundaries to how far you can go. What is your potential?

You came to this planet because there is something you need to do here that is not finished. You are here to live life with potential and purpose; until you discover your reason for living, you have not reached your fullest potential. We were born with a purpose and equipped with potential; we can design our destiny. Fascinating experiences come with potential.

Fear of success

Success is something that you don't just stumble upon. It comes from you having a strong knowledge of what you want and what it takes to accomplish it. Let people know your goals and what you feel inside your soul. Fear can bring integrity and build you up. As you fear your way to success, serve other people; this is going to open up a good opportunity for you. Don't be hard on yourself; as you fear, go forward, be bold, and stand up for yourself and to the media. You are filled with potential. Every successful person had to start off his career with fear; it is a big club, and you are welcome to join—there is no membership required.

Billionaire investor, Warren Buffett, was terrified of public speaking. He was so nervous; he was nervous to speak in front of a crowd. He dropped out of public speaking class before it even started. Mr. Buffett said he lost his nerve. He realized at 21, when he opened his security business in Omaha and decided to reach his full potential, he had to overcome his fear of public speaking.   He enrolled in Dale Carnegie's course. Warren Buffet emphasizes that you have to be able to communicate and talk to others in order to share your ideas and thoughts.

Gold medalist, Michael Phelps, conquered his fear at the age of 7 years; he was scared of putting his face in the water. He mastered the backstroke but later in life was diagnosed with attention deficit hyperactivity disorder (ADHD). He worked his way through this condition with the help of his parents. Michael went on to win 28 medals and become the greatest swimmer in the world

.

"If you want to be the best, you have to do things that other people aren't willing to do."
– Michael Phelps

Fear of the unknown

How many times have you thought about doing something just out of curiosity? You did not even second guess yourself or think about the outcome or the *what if.* You just did it and enjoyed the excitement that went with it. In fact, you wished you would have done it sooner. This was a FEARLESS act on your part, so you can fear the fear.

So, why worry about the unknown? It is not time for that part of our lives to be revealed. Act on the positive side; if you want to buy that house, go for it. Just say, "I can handle it." The same goes for a car or vacation. You can handle it. Fear of justification is what holds many people back from reaching their goals.

"The oldest and strongest emotion of mankind is fear,
and the oldest kind of fear is of the unknown."
– H. P. Lovecraft

REFLECTION OF FEAR

- What do I fear about myself?

- How can I challenge fear?

- How can I address my fear?

COMPASSION

What has happened to compassion? We live in a world where people were once concerned about their family, neighbors, and pets. Now, for decades, people have been asking themselves what has happened to compassion. We see people step on other people's toes and don't apologize, or you may be in line and someone steps in front of you. The worst thing a person can do is lie to your face and, later on, tell you it was just a little white lie—it still hurts your feelings. Have humans lost their touch for compassion?

Researchers reported that there has been a 48% decrease in compassion between 1979 and 2009. Another researcher reported that today's college students were less likely to have compassion for people less fortunate than themselves. What happened to people letting friends vent, and showing moral support for each other? Everyone has a personal opinion, but do they have a listening ear? It is important to keep conversation confidential. You need to understand where a person is coming from and show that you care. What is right or wrong for them may not be right for you; they are confiding in you.

HOW TO SHOW COMPASSION

1. You can be the 1st person to greet someone with a sincere smile.
2. Be mindful how you speak to a person.
3. Complement them on their clothes or hair.
   Look for the good in a person; you will find something nice to say.
4. Send them a thank you card.
5. Have a listening ear, not of your viewpoint but of the other person's.
6. Go out of your comfort zone and meet new friends who are less privileged than you.
7. Always be willing to apologize.

As soon as we, as people, can begin to open our hearts up to people of different cultures, sex, or religions, this world will become one. Goodness is found in all of us.

For more information, go to
www.Revealingwhoyouare.com

NOTES

.

NOTES

NOTES

NOTES

Chapter 4

Stand Up For Yourself

I GOT THIS NO

From the beginning of time and right up till now, the word *no* is a word that many people vision, and dreams are distorted from it. *No* can be something final or shocking to the ears. And nobody wants to be told *No*. *No* is a deal breaker. I recall, when I was 24 years old and single in a one bedroom apartment, I did not fully understand how and why I was getting the rejection of the word *No*. I was seeking a career opportunity, and everywhere I went for a job interview that sounded promising, I would eventually hear *No* again. I was in a state of depression until, one day, I was standing in the middle of my kitchen with the broom in my hand, and a light bulb came on—I understood the word *NO*. It was meant to give me a new meaning in my life. I reversed the two letters to *ON*. It was a better meaning for me: I had to move on, and it was only the end if I wanted it to be. Having a more powerful meaning, the word *ON* gave more hope, courage, and enthusiasm. Nothing could stop me; I embraced my situation. I went back to school and took some computer courses, and engaged in my surroundings. I became happier with myself, and changed my thought process to being open to the word *No* with a smile. It was one of the best life lessons I have ever learned.

EMBRACE NO

No is a powerful word; it makes you think. It makes you change the way you do things in life. You can become more appreciative. Being able to say *No* will help you gain confidence in your life, as well as in your personal standards. Anything is still possible. You can still achieve your dreams. You can love again. You can recover. And you can have peace of mind.

Never fear the word *No*. It is time for you to think how you can overcome the situation. Realize that *no* is a learning experience that you have to handle. And you can have a positive outcome with the word *NO*.

"Let today mark a new beginning for you. Give your permission to say NO without feeling guilty, mean, or selfish. Anybody who gets upset and/or expects you to say YES all of the time, clearly doesn't have your best interest at heart. Always remember: You have a right to say NO, without having to explain yourself. Be at peace with your decisions."
– Stephanie Lahart

Kwesha D. Neal

NOTES

NOTES

NOTES

NOTES

NOTES

Chapter 5

Grab Hold Of Your Vision

GRAB HOLD OF YOUR VISION

The meaning of vision is the state of being able to see ahead of time or something in a dream. Let's go into a time machine, with your genetic code as the password, and explore 5 years in the future; so, get comfortable because you are the navigator —3, 2, 1, blast off! What does it look like? Are you currently pursuing your God-given talent? Are you happy, inside and out, with yourself? Are you fulfilling your purpose? Are you earning the money you deserve? Are you wasting time in a job that does not make you happy?

Do you really believe in your dreams? This your personal opportunity; engage in yourself and what you see in yourself—feel it. Your vision will pull you forward; listen to the conscious voice inside of you and let it guide you in the right direction. Be willing to bring your vision to life. Once you bring it to life, your vision will shine in your business career, and your health will be on the right track.

DREAM FOR DREAM

Have you ever wondered why you had a dream, and you didn't understand the vision of the dream? This dream was bigger than any dream you have ever dreamed before. It was so big that you told your family and friends about it. It was so amazing, you couldn't believe it. In this dream, you saw yourself as being successful, with financial freedom and doing unimaginable things. God created us to have goals and dreams, to move forward and never become stagnant. Everyone has dreams about the life they truly want to live. Some people take a leap of faith to walk into their dreams, while others remain on the sidelines. Just remember: don't ignore your dreams. Your dreams are waiting to come out.

People fail to realize that from the moment they, as humans, are born, they begin to die.

Dreams are important; write them down. You should have a goal each day and accomplish it each day. It could be reading, researching, helping someone, or doing service in your community. Do things you never thought about—live life to the fullest and impact others on your journey.

> "A dream without a positive attitude produces a daydreamer. A positive attitude without a dream produces a pleasant person who can't progress. A dream, together with a positive attitude, produces a person with unlimited possibilities and potential."
> – John C Maxwell

One step at a time

You must lay the foundation for security. This means picking the right business, career, or job.

Then, you must build a wall around your foundation by surrounding yourself with the right circle of people to help you build the wall: good leaders, mentors, and people that love you and care about your future.

There are many options for finding these people: networking, professional career builder organizations, etc.

Then, you need a roof to protect you from the inclement weather.

You must engage with your new friends; have

conviction and let them know you are there for them at all times.

I want to encourage you to press through the hard part because, if you give up, you will never be completely satisfied with yourself.

Every struggle is worth it to fight for your dream. Put on your hard hat because there are going to be times when you are going to get hit upside the head— but this shall pass.

When you complete a task, big or small, you experience a rush of endorphins. You feel happy and motivated. Always find things in life to get excited about.

Investing in Yourself

As I asked in the previous chapters, "Who is more important than YOU?" I know you will answer this by saying that you are. If so, are you really investing in yourself? When we hear the word *investment*, we think of the stock market, mutual funds, buying bonds, or gold. But does this bring you true investment of self-worth? This is not the investment I am talking about. I believe that there is a more important investment, and it gives you greatness beyond what you can imagine.

It is the gift of God's intension that you and I live and enjoy life—physical, emotional, and spiritual health; peace of mind with yourself and your neighbors; personal growth in your joy and happiness—these are your investments that last a lifetime.

This is part of the free will that God gave every one of us on this earth.

And the best thing about this gift, unlike the stock market, is that you don't have to buy this investment or watch the hammer of the stock market hit you on the head. You can sleep at night; this is a worry-free investment. The sky is the limit, and you will always be HAPPY.

Taking it Down

We all need *me-time*—the time when it is okay to do nothing. In fact, if you are a mother, father, or caregiver, you cannot be good at that job if you don't devote some time for yourself. This time allows you to relax and to forget about your worries, and to really focus on yourself and not worry about little Johnnie, the bills, or what happened in the last hour or yesterday. Every day has its own anxieties.

We all know the best things in life are the simple things: having a bubble bath; taking a nap; walking in the park; looking at the blue sky on a bright day; closing your eyes and relaxing in meditation for 10–15 minutes; giving a smile and getting one in return.

Take What You Deserve

I deserve the best, and I accept the best, now.

You deserve more than you expect but, somewhere in your life, the wording was introduced to you in the wrong way.

Here are some affirmations that will help you to believe you deserve the best and more:

- I deserve to be loved.
- I love and approve of myself.
- My actions create constant prosperity
- Wonderful things unfold before me.
- I forgive myself for all the mistakes I have made.
- I replace my anger with understanding and compassion.

Ask yourself: do I really deserve all the above? If so, how can I start to achieve it? What is the first thing I must do to attain it? When you are trying to accomplish goals, know in your conscious mind that it takes time to attain them. Tell your subconscious mind and believe that you have already attained them. Jesus said, "Ask, and you will receive." This is something that was written in the bible over 2000 years ago.

Dress Yourself Up With Your New Investment

I will never try to be someone I am not. We must come to a place where we value ourselves—not from a place of fear but from a place of courage and confidence. Put the most important things in life first.

Ask yourself who else is going to invest in your interests.

Respect who you are and who you are becoming, knowing that you love yourself and God loves you too. It really doesn't matter what society or the culture says about your worth. The only thing that matters is that you believe in your investment in yourself. You are all that you have, and your potential is great.

Your investment can be priceless, e.g., daily walking, jogging, and exercising. Make a daily plan and stick with it. Get the proper amount of sleep (7 to 8 hours). Sleep is good for the brain. Be willing to learn new things in life. Pursue the skills that develop your talent. Find the things that you are naturally good at, and no longer do the things that steal your time and destroy your happiness.

I am in charge of my own destination.

I am on my journey in life. I must reach my destination with my goal.

I know my journey will have steep hills that will come with setbacks, but I am determined to go around the curves. I will climb mountains, even if I need a cane. I will crawl, but I know I will eventually stand. I will get hungry on my journey, but someone will feed me. I will get thirsty, but I will eventually have water from the best spring in life.

"So, come on; reach your destination. Yes, the road is rough, but the rewards are great. We all have dreams; make them come alive. You have seen yourself many times, so follow your destination."
– Kwesha D. Neal

NOTES

NOTES

NOTES

NOTES

Chapter 6

Bring It On

HATERS

For once in my life, I am going to tell you that you need those suckers. This is your biggest entourage; in fact, the more haters, the better. Tell them to get some more people to hate you. Don't give them your power, and don't give up what you love to do.

They gave up on their purpose in life and want you to be like them—that rotten, stinking onion that is scarred and has valueless layers with the disease of *the sea of sameness.* They live a life of dreams in their head, and they don't see with their eyes. Oh, yes, the big procrastinator! I refuse to ride a train that is going nowhere —this life is a journey.

HATER, I AM MOVING ON

There is a saying by Felisha: I have moved on, realizing my gift here on this earth is short. It is estimated that human life expectancy is only 70–80 years. I am full of prosperity, and I have places to go and people to see. I enjoy new experiences that confront me. I accept joy, happiness, a life of abundance, inner peace, and the gift of helping others. I wish haters well.

"I think people are just haters. When they see
People doing well, some people, if there's
something wrong, they'll pick at that."
– Alana Blanchard

YOUR DATA

We previously talked about the brain in Chapter 1. I am going to elaborate just a bit more on the brain: it contains 100 billion neurons, interconnected via trillions of synapses. One single neuron can communicate effectively with thousands of others in a single moment. No computer comes close to the complexity of the brain. The human brain is 30 times faster than the world's best super computer, which is the ISC High Performance. While this computer has an outstanding cooling system, the human brain is exorbitant; when we sleep, it keeps cleaning the cells within us. The brain works 24/7, and it is eager to learn.

It is estimated that we lose about 9,000 neurons a day, but the brain continues to be the fastest computer on the earth. It is amazing, and we have every reason to be happy about our own personal brain, which was made to receive data and obtain memory. While modern technology upgrades computers every few months, your brain transmits new data every day.

WELCOME TO YOUR CONSCIOUS MIND

It is your motion picture in your life that guides you through. Right now, you have a movie playing in your head. It is an amazing movie, and you are the star. It has 4K Ultra HD and the best sound bar for hearing and seeing.

Your movie has smell, hearing, taste, and touch, and you can send your body hunger pains. It also has emotions and memories from when you were a kid, a teenager, and an adult. It is the subject of the mind; we all have our inner voice of awareness.

The person your conscious mind knows best is yourself. Our conscious mind knows our purpose in life, as well as our weaknesses in life. Why do we use our conscious mind? It is the subject of who we are as an individual. Our conscious mind is part of the behavior of the human brain—how we walk, talk, and express ourselves and our life experiences.

The conscious mind is a wonder of life; it brings happiness within itself with spiritual and mental qualities of a lifetime. So, let your *conscious mind* be your guide:

- True happiness, no matter the circumstance in your life.
- Feeling as one with everyone and everything.
- Unconditional love for all living beings.
- Find your biggest *why* in life.
- Permanent, higher shift in your consciousness.

FOUR KEYS TO HAPPINESS

1. Have a spiritual connection with God.

2. Love your neighbor as yourself.

3. Do unto others as you would have them do unto you.

4. There is more happiness in giving than there is in receiving.

These four steps will bring you an abundance of happiness; this is the *happy pill* to life, so live life to the fullest.

The subconscious mind is truly a diamond in the rough. It has a powerful influence over our lives. It is the part of the brain that discovers the power of your beliefs. Over 95% of what we do, think, and say, comes from the subconscious mind, and our mind works day and night. It is also called a homeostatic impulse. The homeostatic impulse keeps your body temperature balanced at 98.6 degrees Fahrenheit. Our bodies maintain a state of homeostasis to ensure our survival.

Your subconscious mind always accepts the domain of two ideas—your conviction without question, whether true or false.

The subconscious mind only thinks of the present, e.g., "I will do something" or "I am going to do something." Your subconscious mind doesn't reason or choose as the conscious mind does. Now is the time to erase those negative sayings that we have programmed in our mind:

- You can't do that.
- You will never amount to anything.
- You must not do that; you are going to fail.
- You can't trust a soul.
- You are too old.
- Nobody cares.

- It's not what you know; it's who you know.
- The world is going to the dogs; what's the use? Nobody cares.

All these negative statements affect the subconscious mind. They bring fear into your heart and mind. This is why we must keep moving in life, set goals, and meditate on the good we see in ourselves.

You must polish your subconscious mind to think in a positive way that opens a new and better *you*.

In my workshop, I encourage my students to open up to the divine guidance of life.

Take five to ten minutes to reflect:

- Divine law and order guides my life.
- Divine action rules my life.
- Divine success is mine.
- Divine harmony is mine.
- Divine peace fills my soul.
- Divine love saturates my whole life.
- Divine abundance is mine.

What else must I do with my *divine*? Share it with everyone I meet!

Every single day of our lives, we are in the progress of improving our subconscious minds; we are polishing up the diamond, which is what we are inside.

You must take your subconscious mind out of its comfort zone and bring on new challenges—your subconscious mind takes risks. Your subconscious mind allows you to feel out of place and to be uncomfortable with new ideas and thoughts. Risk-taking expands our boundaries of comfort. Taking risks is no more detrimental or riskier than playing it safe.

FAILURE allows you to succeed.

Ask yourself questions the brain can't ignore.

- What else is possible for you?
- What do you desire subconsciously? Question your mind.
- What is your expectation for yourself?

Your expectation of yourself is to receive more than what you have received.

- Never come to the conclusion of a negative outcome happening. Step into a positive reality.
- Meditation allows focus on your spiritual being.

- The right side of the brain is the home of the subconscious mind, which brings joy and happiness.

Receiver:

- Teach your subconscious mind that you are the receiver of the thing you wish for or what you want.
- You are born worthy of having.

The subconscious mind is a power house with unlimited riches that can be found there once you have reprogrammed it in your favor; otherwise, you will be a slave to its prior conditions. By allowing yourself to believe in new experiences and possibilities in your life, your thoughts and feelings have intense energy—what you think in your mind and in your body is what you will attract. We all have the positive energy in our mind to fashion a life we desire, such as losing weight, and having great relationships, good health, and fun life experiences.

The subconscious mind has the ability to grow into a massive diamond.

CREATE A NEW CHANGE

Let's make a list of the things you feel are wrong with you, and turn them into positive affirmations.

Just suppose your negative list was something like this:

- I should lose weight.
- Nobody loves me.
- I want to move.
- I hate my job.
- I am not good enough.

Now, turn the list around to be positive affirmations:

- I have a slender body.
- I experience love wherever I go.
- I have a perfect living space.
- I now create a wonderful new job.
- I deserve the best for myself now.

The biggest goal is to approve of who we are and celebrate all new beginnings. As we celebrate this journey through our life, we savor the moments with gratitude and thanksgiving. We accept new affirmations and diligently continue to work on old affirmations. Turn off our conscious mind and let our brain begin to be directed by our subconscious; say yes to our subconscious, without regrets.

NOTES

NOTES

NOTES

NOTES

NOTES

Chapter 7

Go For It

Throughout our childhood and adulthood, we were told by our parents and teachers to be careful, or to be cautious of what we were getting ourselves into. Most of us never asked them why. Immediately, when a person is told something like that, they feel fear; once that happens, you no longer believe in your dream. You no longer have the same thoughts about yourself becoming a lawyer, a doctor, or an astronaut. Many people's careers have been destroyed because of other people's opinions—their dreams became a nightmare.

Don't live a life of regret and be stuck because you let someone else direct your life. We, as humans, were put on this earth to take chances.

As I said in chapter 1, you are the director, producer, and writer of your life. I am telling you, as of today, to go for it! Whether it is your parents, teachers, girlfriend, boyfriend, wife, or husband—never let anyone tell your story. Your story consists of your vision, your happiness, your goals, and your prosperity.

As of today, I am going tell you to live your story. This is part of your progress in the purpose of your life. Take control of your authority, and work hard for what is rendered to you.

- Take action.
- Be patient with yourself.
- Set a schedule.
- Make a monthly goal for yourself.
- Engage with people on the same path.

You will only receive this gift of life once; make good decisions, and enjoy it every day.

TRULY LIVING

What does it mean to truly live? It is the feeling of making the right decisions for yourself, and no longer blaming others for your past mistakes. You stop making excuses for your lack of initiative. You never second guess or doubt yourself, or have a lack of conviction for what makes you happy. At any given time, you can voice your opinion. You have given up on the game of pleasing everyone around you in order to make them like you. You have your uniqueness, and you love it. You are the valuable person God created you to be.

The very best life is to truly live life without confusion, pain, or paralysis.

Set your mind to be agreeable with your heart. The more progress you make, the fewer bad days you will have. You have to keep moving.

You don't wish your life away waiting for the weekend. You live every day of your life as if it were the weekend.

In my workshop, I informed my clients that every day they rise up out of bed, it should be like the weekend—you should have fun every day. Even if you only spend one hour doing something you love, it is that feeling of goodness, and that feeling of freedom— it's that *wow factor* of being happy. You will push yourself to have a winning attitude. And you will want the world to know you are changing in a good way. I know who I have become: bold, confident, courageous, and unafraid to try new things.

Tell yourself that anything you love doing that is productive and consists of you, is priceless.

For more information, go to
www.Revealingwhoyouare.com.

TIME

We all have heard and said it before: if only I had more time. Yes, I know there is 24 hours in a day, and 168 hours per week, and 365 days in a year; it still isn't enough time. No one can buy time. No one can store time. Once it is gone, it is gone forever. But time is our best friend. With time, we keep appointments. We know what time it is. The earth is moving, so time brings forth a new day. The problem is, we don't value our time. We procrastinate what we can do today until tomorrow; in other words, we are borrowing from Peter to pay Paul. You don't really pay for things with money; you pay for them with time.

Questions you may ask yourself about time:

- If it takes me such a long time to make a decision, how important could this matter be?

- Am I going to allow procrastination to rob me of the joy of time?

- Do I value my time?

THE POWER OF FOCUS

Focus is the key that determines your success or failure. Focus is an act of concentrating with interest. The average human has an eight-second attention span, less than that of a goldfish, according to a 2015 study by Microsoft.

Your focus drives your thoughts and emotions. When you focus on your passion so intently, it gives you the adrenaline of accomplishment. Stay on your path because, once you get off, it is hard to get back on your path. It is OK to say yes sometime to things that you are not focused on, but don't schedule too much on your calendar that will take you away from those things. Picture yourself running; you are in a marathon, and you are giving all you have. You see yourself cross the finish line. Once you cross the finish line, the door of opportunity opens for you.

Here are some tips that will help you stay focused:

1. Write out your goal. This is the 1st step in goal setting.
2. Create a mission statement. This helps you direct your time and energy toward things that matter.

3. Count your time. Prioritize what is important or urgent.
4. Develop milestones toward your goals. Create milestones that will help you move toward you goal without losing focus.
5. Have a game plan to help achieve your goals.
6. Analyze your process on a daily basis. Every goal should be tracked on a daily basis.
7. Avoid procrastination; this kills your time.
8. Implement motivational techniques; this will help you stay on track.

STEPPING INTO YOUR GREATNESS

Without a shadow of doubt, your greatness is much bigger than you are. Many outstanding people don't take the time to look at all the outstanding qualities that they possess. These are beautiful qualities that don't require a bachelor degree, master's degree, or doctorate degree. In fact, Jesus didn't have a degree, but he was the greatest teacher on earth. He was a carpenter. And he didn't feel any less than people who received their degree. Jesus set many good examples for us. He even died for all of us so that we may have a better life. You need to remind yourself of your greatness.

When you move forward, no longer afraid of hurt or failure, and stop breathing life into your insecurities, then your greatness can appear. Your life becomes a series of events of happiness and great moments. The more greatness, the more gifts of greatness: enormous, radiant, great joy and love. You are who you become— a person of greatness.

These are ways to step into greatness:

- Be present – whatever you are doing, wherever you are, be all there.

- Show up – lead by example and respect other people's time.

- Confidence – Take great pride in what you do and be proud of who you are.

- Keep Integrity – Make the decision in life to always do what is best for your life.

- Give to others – Look at how you can contribute to other's success and happiness.

LIVING WITH REGRET

Let us first understand what regret is. It is an emotional state that involves blaming ourselves for a bad outcome. People carry regret very heavily in their mind and in their heart. We go through life with regret that can deter painful experiences.

We are all busy. Life gets in the way, and things happen that lead to regrets; for example, working so much instead of spending time with our friends and family and sharing a lasting laugh.

Not having true confidence in ourselves, we can spend a great portion of our lives being worried about what other people think of us. Having good people in our lives is what matters.

Sometimes we live a life that our parents want us to live instead of the one we want to live. Parents are good role models, but they must let their kids live with free will and develop into the person that they choose to be, and let them choose their own career. If kids choose to live in the shell of their parents, they will never leave the cocoon and be the beautiful butterfly.

Trusting that voice in the back of my head: most of us have experienced a little voice in the back our head giving us the sign, *don't do it.* But instead, we do it and find out later that it was not a good decision. Here are some examples: taking a job just to have a job; or marrying a person that you know is not right for you.

Spending more time with the kids: It is stated that it is not the quantity of time that's important; it's the quality of time. It is estimated that a mother gives her kids less than 15 minutes of quality time a day, and a father less than 10 minutes of quality time. We get too busy working, staying late at the office and, on the weekends, we try to make up for it with our kids by taking them to basketball or baseball practice.

EASE THOSE REGRETS

"I regret those times when I've chosen the dark side. I've wasted enough time not being happy."
– Jessica Lange

For godly grief produces a repentance that leads to salvation without regret, whereas worldly grief produces death.
(2 Corinthians 7:10)

When you find yourself focusing on regrets, here are some things you can do:

- Think about what lesson you learned.

- Think about what wisdom you gained.

- Set new goals for yourself that are positive and meaningful.

I'd like to tell you a story about a trip. The story goes like this: I didn't plan on taking a trip this time of year. I found myself packing in a hurry for the trip. I knew it was going to be an unpleasant trip and no good was going to come out of it. I got a ticket to fly on *Wish Airline.* I kept my baggage with me. I couldn't check it because it was weighed down with a thousand memories. I entered the *Regret International Airport.* I say *international* because people from all over the world come here.

As I checked into the last city hotel, I noticed that it was hosting a pity patty party, and many citizens were going to be there.

I first met the *Done* family: I Have Done, Could Have Done, and I Am Done With It.

Then I met the *Had* family: I Had This and I Had That.

The biggest family was *Yesterday*: there were too many to count, but each one would have their story about what happened yesterday and would never move to the next day with a new plan.

Then there was the *Scattered Dream* family: Dreams that make dreams that have fear in themselves.

Then there was the *Fail* family: they told us stories about things that have failed in their lives (careers, marriages, foreclosures, and bankruptcies).

To make a long story short, I went to this same party knowing that there would not be any benefits in going. As usual, I became depressed; but as in all the stories of failure brought back from the past, I realized that this pity party trip could be cancelled by me, and I would leave once and for all.

City of Regret: I would not leave a forwarding address. Yes, I am sorry for the mistake I made in the past. I forgive myself, and will start a new life. I am asking you to move forward and take up a new residence where you are surrounded by positivity and smiles. You don't have to carry around heavy luggage loaded with sorrow and regrets—give it to God. And if you choose to carry your regrets all of your days, this is your personal decision. A burdened shoulder will lead to poor health and unhappiness. So, at my request, I am asking you to give up on your regrets.

For more information, go to
www.Revealingwhoyouare.com.

NOTES

NOTES

NOTES

NOTES

About the Author

Kwesha Denice Neal was born in Newark, New Jersey. She attended Essex County College where she obtained a Programming Certificate. Later, she attended Structure Network in Jersey City, where she studied Cisco Systems.

Kwesha traveled five continents, exploring different cultures and customs. She volunteered at Ezulwini Charity Initiative Programmes in Swaziland, South Africa, and understands that the meaning of life is happiness, serving others, and finding purpose, and that she could not do anything on this earth by herself.

Kwesha Denice Neal became very passionate about reaching her true potential in her life, so she hired a life coach, and was able to see the wonderful results and the transformation in her life. Throughout the process, she has excelled with a higher potential for growth.

In 2016, she became a certified John Maxwell coach. Kwesha Denice Neal is happy adding values and connecting with people of all cultures. Kwesha Denice Neal is directing her coaching knowledge of the core process that is essential to life.

In 2017, she joined the MOBE family to help small business owners and entrepreneurs launch, run, and grow their own highly successful business.